THE DISCOVERY OF THE AMERICAS

ACTIVITIES BOOK

➤ ENCOURAGES HANDS-ON LEARNING:

The more children *do*, the more they enjoy learning and the more they learn!

➤ CAN BE TAILORED TO *YOUR* NEEDS:

Included are projects for the whole class, small groups, and individuals. Children can work in a structured setting or independently, in the classroom or for extra credit. Teacher participation is up to *you*!

➤ IS FLEXIBLE:

Projects can be done in a few hours or over many days and are designed for a wide range of abilities and interests.

➤ CAN BE USED YEAR AFTER YEAR:

Each page is marked for cutting and hole punching. Insert the pages into a standard three-ring binder for a permanent student-activities resource.

➤ CONTAINS FULL INSTRUCTIONS FOR PUPILS:

Cut them out and slip them into a three-ring binder and/or post them prominently so that children can refer to them at any time.

➤ MAKES LEARNING FUN AND INTERESTING:

You'll find your pupils returning to these activities again and again, year after year.

Betsy and Giulio Maestro

THE DISCOVERY
OF
THE AMERICAS

ACTIVITIES BOOK

LOTHROP, LEE & SHEPARD BOOKS
NEW YORK

Contents

THE ACTIVITIES

THE DISCOVERY OF THE AMERICAS
ACTIVITIES BOOK
A Hands-On Cross-Curriculum Approach

Using These Activities with Your Class

A GUIDE FOR TEACHERS

The book *The Discovery of The Americas* will introduce many students to some new ideas and concepts. The projects in this Activities Book, which is designed to be used with *The Discovery of The Americas*, will help children see that history is made up of connected events, not isolated incidents. The voyages of Columbus comprise only one chapter of the longer story of America's discovery.

These activities can be used in the way that best suits your particular classroom situation. Most of the activities can be done individually or by small groups. Some are appropriate as whole-class activities. Whereas some of the activities may require a number of weeks to complete, others may be finished in just a day or two. Most call for easy-to-find materials or none at all. Although some teacher guidance and supervision are essential, most students in grades three and up should be able to be fairly independent. In grades one and two, teachers will want to offer more assistance. Some children will, of course, work above or below their grade level, depending on their interests and skills. **The easiest activities are marked with a single diamond; moderate ones with two diamonds; more difficult or complex ones with three.**

The pages are marked for placement in a three-ring binder so that students can choose and participate in the activities on their own. The instructions can be enlarged and posted for display as well as being placed in a binder or permanent casing of your choice.

Parents and caregivers will also find many of these projects fun and interesting activities for the home.

Many areas of the curriculum can be enriched by these activities. Language Arts, Reading, Social Studies, Science, Math, and Art are all involved. Various study skills will be practiced; using reference materials, taking notes, and doing research are an intregal part of most of the activities. The writing process is an important aspect of many activities as well. Naturally, map and globe study go hand in hand with the use of the book and the activities. Creative thinking and the use of problem-solving skills are essential to all of these activities, and children should be encouraged to approach them with active imaginations.

In working on these activities, **your students will be active participants in the learning process**. This is particularly important in the teaching of history, a subject that so many people seem to find dull or boring. It is my hope that both the book and the activities will be useful additions to your existing curriculum and will contribute to making this period of our history exciting to your students. If we can make history fun and interesting for kids—make it come alive—they will be enthusiastic learners. As their understanding of history grows, they will be capable of a better understanding of the world today and better able to participate in shaping its future.

Betsy Maestro

How to Work On These Activities

A GUIDE FOR STUDENTS

1. Read through the whole activity carefully.

2. Make a plan for working on the activity. Make a list of the things you will need to do. If you are working in a group, each person should have something to do.

3. You will probably need to look at some other books to get more information. Go to the library in your school or neighborhood. If you can't find what you need, ask your teacher or librarian for help.

4. Gather your information. Look over the books or other materials you found. Do some reading. Make some notes or little pictures to help you remember the information you need.

5. If you will be writing, make a rough, or "working," copy first. Read it over to find mistakes and to make any changes that are needed. Have another person read it over, too. He or she may have some good suggestions. Then you will be ready to make your final copy.

6. Remember to make a sketch or plan for any artwork you will be doing. Work lightly in pencil first. Then you can make changes before you darken it or add color.

7. If you will be performing live or on tape, make sure you practice first. Allow time for rehearsals.

8. Take pride in your project! It's yours—show what a good job you can do! Following all of these steps will help make your project the best that it can be.

Give America a New Name

You can do this by yourself or in a small group

Text © 1992 by Betsy Maestro   Illustrations © 1991, 1992 by Giulio Maestro   Printed in USA

Focus Activity / Naming the New World

Give America a New Name

You can do this by yourself or in a small group

The name "America" was a mistake. Mapmakers thought that Amerigo Vespucci had been the first to discover these new lands. So they named them after him. If North America had been named for Christopher Columbus instead, perhaps you would live on a continent named Columbia or Columbiana.

What if the New World had been named for Leif Ericsson or the Vikings? What might it have been called? It could also have been named for John Cabot, Saint Brendan, or Magellan. What names might have been used if the New World had been named for them?

The Americas probably already had many names when these explorers first came to the New World. What names might the first Americans have given to these lands? Sometimes names for places come from the way they look. Greenland got its name because the land there looked so green. Why was Newfoundland a good name? Think up as many different names for America as you can. Write them down and share them with the class.

Focus Activity / Naming the New World

◆

Be a Printer

You can do this by yourself or with a partner

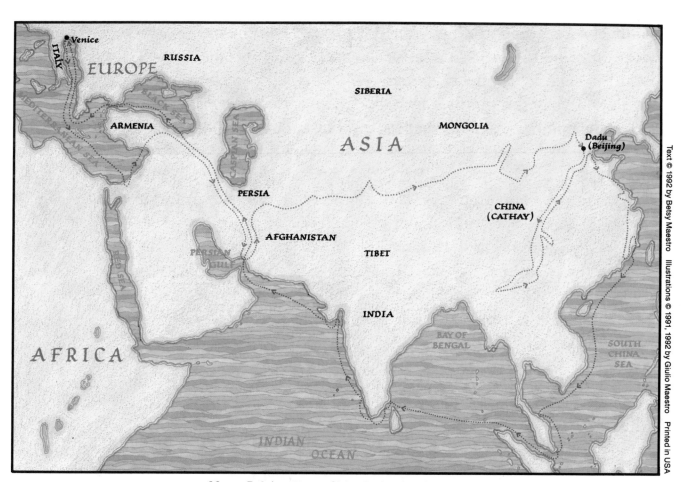

Marco Polo's route to China by land and sea

Text © 1992 by Betsy Maestro   Illustrations © 1991, 1992 by Giulio Maestro   Printed in USA

Focus Activity / Chinese Block Printing

◆

Be a Printer

You can do this by yourself or with a partner

Printing is a way of making many copies of the same thing quickly. Books, magazines, and newspapers are printed. Long ago, the Chinese invented block printing. This was a very simple kind of printing, done by hand. Today, most printing is done using very large machines.

You can do your own block printing. First, you must make a printing block. Rubber erasers, sponges, firm fruits or vegetables cut in half (apples or potatoes are good—tomatoes are not!), or soft wood make good blocks. You can draw your design onto the block, or you can work "free hand." Use a metal or wooden tool (an old screwdriver, a butter knife, or an unsharpened pencil are all possibilities) to cut or dig out your design. By carefully digging out parts, you can make letters or numbers, simple shapes or pictures, or other designs.

Dip your printing block into paint or ink. Now, press it onto paper or cloth. Use color, be imaginative, and have fun! How many prints can you make with one dipping? Make as many blocks as you want. You may want to use a separate color for each one.

You may want to make a small book using your printing blocks. Did your letters or numbers come out backward? Did you discover the trick? Keep trying and you'll work it out.

You might find it interesting to read about block printing. Find out how the Chinese first did it.

piece of potato

cut away

paint in tray

printed design

Focus Activity / Chinese Block Printing

◆

Put On a Puppet Show

Do this in a small group

Text © 1992 by Betsy Maestro   Illustrations © 1991, 1992 by Giulio Maestro   Printed in USA

Focus Activity / Famous Explorers

◆
Put On a Puppet Show

Do this in a small group

Make some simple stick or paper-bag puppets of Columbus, Cabot, Vespucci, Balboa, and Magellan. Pretend that these famous explorers have gotten together to talk about their voyages. Plan what each one will say. Perhaps they will tell what they saw. They may talk about an interesting thing that happened on their trip. Maybe they will argue about whose discoveries were the most important.

Each of you will need to learn a little about the explorer you will be speaking for. Make sure you know enough to make your conversation interesting. Have a few rehearsals before you perform your show for the rest of your class. Remember to use your imaginations! Your puppets might have funny stories or jokes to tell about their voyages.

Stick Puppet

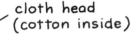

cloth head
(cotton inside)

← string or
rubber band

←popsicle or
other stick

glued-on
yarn hair

← painted face

← cloth cape

For a larger puppet
use a paper bag

head
stuffed
with
shredded
paper

← stick

◆

Be a Famous Person

You can do this by yourself

Text © 1992 by Betsy Maestro   Illustrations © 1991, 1992 by Giulio Maestro   Printed in USA

Whole-Book Activity / People Who Participated in Discovery

Be a Famous Person

You can do this by yourself

Choose a person from the book *The Discovery of The Americas*. It can be anyone from Leif Ericsson or Marco Polo to Queen Isabella or Ferdinand Magellan. Find out what your person wore. You will need to look at some other books. Make a simple costume and dress up as this person. You can make your outfit out of cloth or paper or you can use old dress-up clothes from home. You might just make a few items to wear over your own clothes—such as a shield or cape, helmet or hat.

Tell the class who you are and what you are famous for. Remember to tell when and where you lived. The class may have some questions for you. Be sure you know enough about your person to answer questions. You'll need to have a good imagination, too!

◆ ◆

What Am I Eating?

You can do this by yourself or in a small group

Text © 1992 by Betsy Maestro   Illustrations © 1991, 1992 by Giulio Maestro   Printed in USA

Focus Activity / Foods of the New World

◆ ◆
What Am I Eating?

You can do this by yourself or in a small group

Many fruits and vegetables growing in the New World were unknown to the Europeans who first went there. Corn, potatoes, peppers, and squash are some of them. Pretend you are eating these foods for the first time. Describe them to your class. Tell how each one looks. What does it smell and taste like? How does it feel to the touch? See if the class can guess what this new food is from your clues.

Use your library and see if you can find out about some other foods that were new to the Europeans. Some will surprise you! One is something yummy—a real treat! The sailors took these new things home with them. Many became so popular that it is hard to imagine how Europeans lived without them. Can you imagine Italians with no tomato sauce?

◆ ◆

Be a Native Artist

You can do this by yourself or with a partner

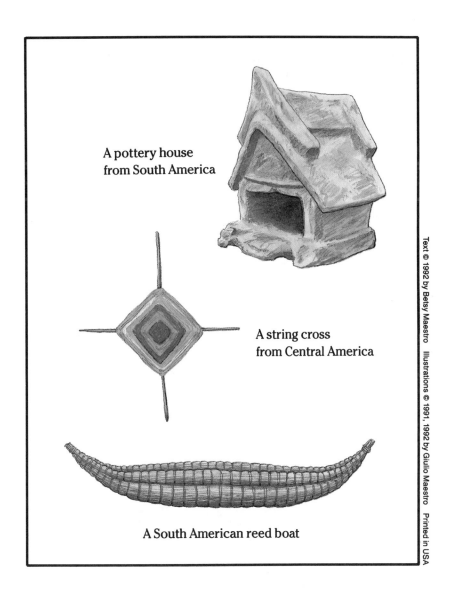

A pottery house
from South America

A string cross
from Central America

A South American reed boat

Focus Activity / Native American Art

◆ ◆
Be a Native Artist

You can do this by yourself or with a partner

Make your own piece of look-alike Native American art. You may use any material you like: clay, cloth, wood, straw, bark, paper. You can probably think of other materials, too. You can make a simple book, a pot, a bowl, a design, a mask, or a weaving. You will need to look at some pictures of these objects in books. And you may be able to visit a museum that has some Native American objects or works of art.

Once you have seen some examples, you can plan your own art piece. After you have completed it, write a few sentences telling what your object is and what it is used for.

◆ ◆ ◆

What Will You Need?

You can do this by yourself or in a small group

Focus Activity / Planning for a Voyage

◆ ◆ ◆

What Will You Need?

You can do this by yourself or in a small group

It's your job to outfit one of Magellan's ships. This means that you must decide what things you will need on your voyage. Think about what you might need on such a long trip. You will have to plan on a supply of food, tools, weapons, and extra parts for your ship. What other kinds of things will be needed?

Think about what would be truly necessary—things that you must have. Then think about what other items would be useful or just nice to have along. There may be some items that you could get along the way; can you think of any?

Use your imagination as much as possible. You can look at some books to get other ideas. Remember that space on your ship is limited: not everything you could use will fit. You must plan carefully. There won't be any shops along the way, and you don't want to run out of the really important supplies—such as food! Be ready to present your list of supplies to the captain for approval.

Find the Places

You can do this in a small group or with your whole class

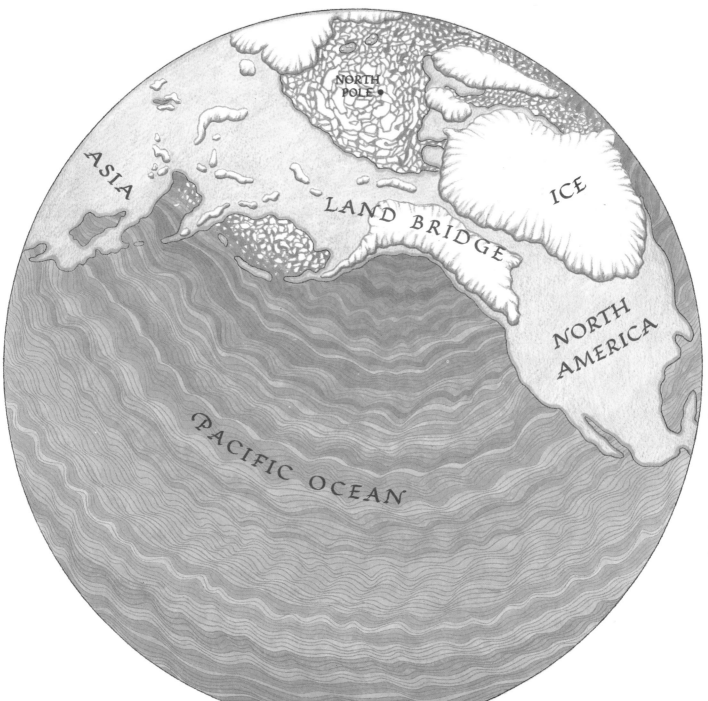

Text © 1992 by Betsy Maestro   Illustrations © 1991, 1992 by Giulio Maestro   Printed in USA

Whole-Book Activity / Understanding Maps and Globes

◆ Find the Places

You can do this in a small group or with your whole class

Use a world map and a globe to find the places in the book *The Discovery of The Americas*. Where was the land bridge from Asia? Where were the Mayan cities? Where was Vinland? Go on through the book and end with the ship *Victoria*'s return to Spain. Use pins or colored paper or removable stickers to mark each location.

Now see if you can trace the routes of some of the famous voyages. What routes did Columbus follow? How about John Cabot? Use fine string or colored ribbon to show the routes. See if you can find out how many miles some of the explorers traveled.

◆

You're the Teacher!

Do this by yourself or with one or two partners

Text © 1992 by Betsy Maestro   Illustrations © 1991, 1992 by Giulio Maestro   Printed in USA

Concluding Activity / New Vocabulary

◆
You're the Teacher!

Do this by yourself or with one or two partners

Pretend that you're the teacher. You want to make up a spelling test for your class using new words found in *The Discovery of The Americas*. Go through the whole book. Find ten or more new words. Try to find words that will be right for your class. Choose words that may be a little hard—but not so difficult that no one will be able to spell them!

Make a list of the words. Write a definition, or meaning, next to each word. Ask your teacher if you can give your test to the whole class or maybe just to one group. You may assign a different word to each person. Or you may want to give everyone the whole list. Have the kids spell each word and use it in a sentence if they can. See how well they do. Talk about any words that they didn't know. How was your test? Was it too hard? Too easy? Just right?

Headline! Read All About It!

You can do this by yourself or in a small group

Text © 1992 by Betsy Maestro   Illustrations © 1991, 1992 by Giulio Maestro   Printed in USA

Whole-Book Activity / Important Events

Headline! Read All About It!

You can do this by yourself or in a small group

"COLUMBUS SIGHTS LAND!" could have been a newspaper headline on October 12, 1492. Headlines should be short and exciting. They catch the reader's eye. They make the reader want to know more. Headlines make people want to read the stories in the newspaper.

Using the events in this book, see if you can write some exciting headlines. "MARCO POLO REACHES CHINA!" could be one. See if you can come up with at least ten different headlines for the "news events" in the book.

It might be fun to choose your favorite headline and write the rest of the news story to go with it. You should try to tell what happened in about ten sentences. A news story should tell: *who* was there, *what* happened, *where* it happened, and *when*. If you are working in a group, each person can pick a story to write. Then you'll have a whole newspaper!

Whole-Book Activity / Important Events

◆◆

Ask an Explorer

You can do this by yourself

Whole-Book Activity / Explorer Interview

Ask an Explorer

You can do this by yourself

Reporters are people who write about the day's events for newspapers and magazines. Pretend that you are a reporter. Make believe that you have a chance to talk to one of the explorers from *The Discovery of The Americas.* Whom will you choose? Pick someone who seems interesting to you. You can interview the explorer you choose. You'll ask the questions and the explorer will answer.

Make up a list of questions you would like to ask. You should think of at least five. You might ask about the voyage. You could find out about the explorer's life: Where does he come from? Does he have any children? You could ask about what he saw in the New World. Would he like to live there?

Write your questions down. Then write down the answers that the explorer might give you. You can use your imagination, and you can also read a little about this person. Then you will really know what the explorer might have told you. Since you can't take a photo of your explorer, draw a little picture of him to go with your interview.

◆

Make Your Own Alphabet Book

You can do this by yourself or in a small group

Text © 1992 by Betsy Maestro   Illustrations © 1991, 1992 by Giulio Maestro   Printed in USA

Whole-Book Activity / Discovery ABC

◆
Make Your Own Alphabet Book

You can do this by yourself or in a small group

Make a *Discovery of The Americas* alphabet book. For each letter of the alphabet, find a person, place, or thing that is part of the discovery of the New World. You can use words from this book and other books. Here are some ideas for *A* words to get you started: Americas, adventure, Atlantic, Aztecs, Adena, Anasazi, archaeologist, Amerigo. Can you find any others? Now find words for letters *B* to *Z*. Which letter do you think will be the easiest? Which will be the hardest?

When you have picked out a word for each letter, you can make your book. Make a page for each letter. Write the word and make a picture to go with it. Know something about each word you choose. Use color to make your book look really nice.

Your whole class could make an alphabet "quilt." Each person can choose a letter to make. Use small squares of paper or fabric. Put a letter, word, and picture on each. Then the twenty-six squares can be glued, taped, or sewn together to make the quilt.

◆ ◆

Write with Pictures

You can do this by yourself or in a small group

Focus Activity / Written Language

♦ ♦

Write with Pictures

You can do this by yourself or in a small group

The Maya had a whole written language. Many people long ago had ways of writing with small pictures or symbols. A picture of a bird could be used to mean *bird*. Some people used pictures or symbols to stand for parts of words. Or they could stand for sounds, the way the letters of our alphabet do. Different people had different ways of writing.

See if you can make up your own simple written language. You decide what pictures or symbols you will use. You might just have symbols for important words. You might make a small picture of a sun to stand for *sun* or *light*. Or you can make symbols for each sound of your language. A small picture of a turtle might stand for the sound that our letter *T* makes. Make a key—a list of the symbols and what they mean.

Use your symbols to write a story in just a few sentences. See if others in your class can figure out what it says.

◆ ◆

Who Am I?
A Game of Twenty Questions

You can do this in a small group or with your whole class

Text © 1992 by Betsy Maestro   Illustrations © 1991, 1992 by Giulio Maestro   Printed in USA

Whole-Book Activity / Notable People

Who Am I?
A Game of Twenty Questions

You can do this in a small group or with your whole class

This game may be played with the whole class or with a smaller group. Each player, in turn, pretends to be an important person. This person must be someone who had a part in the discovery of the New World. Pick someone that the class read about in *The Discovery of The Americas*. The rest of the class or group must try to guess who the person is. They will do this by asking questions. The questions may only be answered with YES or NO.

Only twenty questions may be asked. Each questioner may make a guess. At the end, the whole group must guess who the person is.

Each player should know enough about the person to be able to answer the questions correctly. A good way to make sure that no two players will pretend to be the same person is to write the name of each person from the book on a slip of paper. Then one slip can be given to each player. Make sure that each one keeps the name of the person a secret! Then play the game and see if you can stump the rest of your class.

Pretend You're a Hunter

Do this by yourself or in a small group

Focus Activity / Hunters in Ancient America

◆
Pretend You're a Hunter

Do this by yourself or in a small group

Pretend that you are part of a tribe of nomads living thousands of years ago. These people hunted large animals for food. They had very few tools and no horses. They had to hunt on foot. They hunted in groups. Use your imagination. Think about what animals you might hunt. How might you kill an animal? How would you eat it? Write a short story about a recent hunt you went on. Draw a picture of the large animal you killed. Show what weapons or tools you used.

Do a little reading about these people. See if you can discover which animals they actually hunted. Find out what weapons they had. Tell the class about what you learned. Was your own story very different from what you read about?

◆ ◆

Be a Travel Agent

You can do this by yourself or with a partner

Text © 1992 by Betsy Maestro   Illustrations © 1991, 1992 by Giulio Maestro   Printed in USA

Focus Activity/ The New World

◆ ◆
Be a Travel Agent

You can do this by yourself or with a partner

Many explorers have returned to Europe raving about the wonders of a fabulous new place that they call the New World. You are a travel agent and you want to encourage your customers to be the first tourists in the New World.

Prepare a fold-out brochure with several pages, telling about this new vacation spot. Naturally, since there are no hotels or resorts yet, you will have to sell the idea of the "rustic comfort of grass huts..." and so on. This project can be done in a fun and humorous way, but be sure to include some real information about what these tourists might see in the places they would be visiting. Describe the scenery, the recreational possibilities, the food, and the people of the New World. What purchases might these tourists be able to make? What souvenirs could they take home? Use exciting language and colorful pictures in your brochure to attract your customers. Share it with the class.

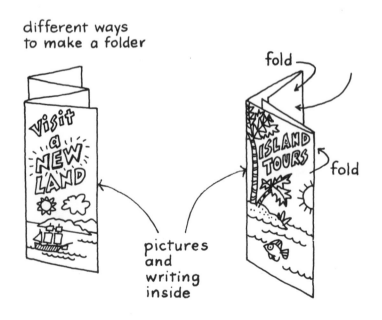

Focus Activity/ The New World

What Did They See?

You can do this by yourself or with a partner

Text © 1992 by Betsy Maestro   Illustrations © 1991, 1992 by Giulio Maestro   Printed in USA

Focus Activity / Comparative Geography

◆ ◆
What Did They See?

You can do this by yourself or with a partner

Explorers and sailors left their families and friends at home while they traveled. When they returned, they told what they had seen and done. But since not all of them saw the same things, not all the reports were the same. Travelers who took a northern route saw what is now Canada. Those who sailed a southern route saw islands in the Caribbean Sea and parts of Central and South America. Christopher Columbus saw a different New World from the one that John Cabot saw.

Pretend that you are Columbus. Write a letter home telling about the places you have visited. Tell about the weather and climate. Is it cold or hot? Describe some plants and animals that you see. What do the native people wear? Why?

Now pretend that you are John Cabot. Write a letter telling about what you saw. What's the temperature like in the far north? What is the land like? How are the natives dressed? Why? What kinds of trees are there? What kinds of animals?

It will be interesting to see how different these two letters about the New World are. Which place would seem better to you? Tell why.

◆

Make a Set of Stamps

You can do this by yourself or with a partner

Text © 1992 by Betsy Maestro   Illustrations © 1991, 1992 by Giulio Maestro   Printed in USA

Focus Activity / Great Explorer Postage Stamps

Make a Set of Stamps

You can do this by yourself or with a partner

Pretend that the U.S. Postal Service has asked you to design a new series of stamps, called "The Great Explorers." The set will include four to six new stamps to honor these brave men. Each stamp will be a picture of a well-known explorer. Some stamps may also show the ships from these famous voyages. Each stamp can have its own size and design.

Make your stamps colorful and pleasing to look at. Do not try to make them actual size. The artists who design real stamps make large designs. Later the picture is made small enough for a postage stamp. So make your stamp design in a size that you are comfortable with. Don't forget to put the postage amount in cents and the letters USA in your design. It will help to look at some real stamps before you get started.

How Did They Get Here?

You can do this by yourself or with a partner

Text © 1992 by Betsy Maestro   Illustrations © 1991, 1992 by Giulio Maestro   Printed in USA

Focus Activity / Transportation

◆
How Did They Get Here?

Some people came to the New World on foot—wandering across the land bridge. Later, people came by boat and by ship. Some came to stay. Others came to explore. It is possible that there were some visitors that we don't know about. Use your imagination to make up a story about some visitors to the New World. Who were they? Where did they come from? What part of the New World did they visit?

Tell about what they saw and did here. Perhaps they met some interesting native people. Maybe they saw odd animals and plants. They probably tried some new foods. Think about what might have happened to them. Why did they leave here? Did they just go back to their homes? Write your story down.

Make a picture to go with your story. Show how your people got to the New World.

Now make another picture showing how some others really arrived. You might show a Viking ship or a big sailing ship that came around the time of Columbus.

How do you think people would come to America today? You could make a picture of that, too.

◆ ◆

Signal that Ship!

You can do this by yourself or in a small group

Text © 1992 by Betsy Maestro   Illustrations © 1991, 1992 by Giulio Maestro   Printed in USA

◆ ◆
Signal that Ship!

You can do this by yourself or in a small group

On many voyages of discovery, there were a number of ships traveling together. Columbus had three ships on his first journey, and Magellan had five. Sometimes the captain of one ship needed to tell the other captains something important. Maybe there was something wrong with his ship. Maybe someone had spotted land. Radios and telephones had not yet been invented. How do you think they communicated with one another?

Think about this problem. Write down some ideas. See if you can come up with some ways they could have signaled each other. Suppose you had to make your own set of signals for the ships. Maybe you would have just a few signals for important messages such as "Help!" or "Land Sighted!" or "Man Overboard!" Or would you have a signal for each letter of the alphabet and spell each word out? Some signals can be heard—such as bells. Other signals are meant to be seen—such as flags or lights. What kind would you use?

Focus Activity / Communication

◆ ◆

You Are There!

Do this with a group

Whole-Book Activity / Historic Events

21

◆ ◆
You Are There!

Do this with a group

You are there! Pretend that you are on the scene at the exact moment of a great discovery. You are there when Balboa sights the Pacific Ocean for the first time. Or you are there when John Cabot first sees the coast of Newfoundland. Or you are there when some of the very earliest "Americans" first reach the tip of South America. Write a short play about this event. Give the details of the story as it is happening. You can do some reading and use as much real information as you want. Or you can just imagine what may have happened.

A narrator or storyteller can tell some of what is happening. Some of the story can be told through conversation and action. Some people in the group can act out parts. You will need to write down what they will say. If you want to, you can make some scenery and wear simple costumes.

When your play is ready, have a few rehearsals, or practices. Then you'll be ready to perform! Perform your play in front of the class. Or record it with a video camera and show your tape to the class.

◆ ◆

You Make the Rules

You can do this by yourself or in a small group

Text © 1992 by Betsy Maestro   Illustrations © 1991, 1992 by Giulio Maestro   Printed in USA

Focus Activity / Rules and Laws

You Make the Rules

You can do this by yourself or in a small group

Anytime a group of people are together, there need to be some rules. Rules help people know how to behave. Rules set limits for the group. Then each person knows what he or she is allowed to do and what he or she is not allowed to do.

Different rules are needed for different groups. Your rules at home are not the same as your rules in school. If you play sports on a team, you may have to follow other rules. Grown-ups have lots of rules to follow, too. Cities, states, and countries have rules or laws that all people must follow or obey. There may be punishments for people who do not obey rules or laws.

Pretend that you are the captain of a ship on a voyage of discovery. You must make a list of rules for your crew to follow while you are at sea. Divide your list into Dos and Don'ts. Decide what things your crew should do and should not do. Think about rules that will make it easier for everyone to get along. Make rules that will be fair and will help the crew members to treat each other with respect. How will you make sure that the crew will obey the rules? What will you do if someone breaks the rules?

What's in that Time Capsule?

You can do this by yourself or in a small group

Pottery pieces
from South America

A dog on wheels
from Central America

A stone fishhook from the
west coast of North America

Text © 1992 by Betsy Maestro   Illustrations © 1991, 1992 by Giulio Maestro   Printed in USA

Focus Activity / Life in the Ancient Americas

What's in that Time Capsule?

You can do this by yourself or in a small group

Imagine that you have found a time capsule from the ancient Americas. It was buried deep in the earth and you have uncovered it. It is an extremely important find. After you've had a chance to study the objects inside, it will be your job to write a description of each of the items. This information will go to other archaeologists. Make a drawing of each object as well. They will want to see what these artifacts look like.

The objects in the time capsule might include such things as pottery, utensils, jewelry, toys, masks, figurines. There may be writing or pictures drawn on some objects that would give additional clues about the way these ancient people may have lived. Tell what each object looks like: its size, shape, and color. Tell what it was probably used for. See what you can guess about the people who used it. After you have looked at all the objects, what would you be able to say about the kind of life these people lived?

You will be able to get ideas for this project by looking at pictures of ancient artifacts in some library books. You might be able to visit a museum that has these kinds of objects on display.

Be a Game Creator

You can do this by yourself or in a small group

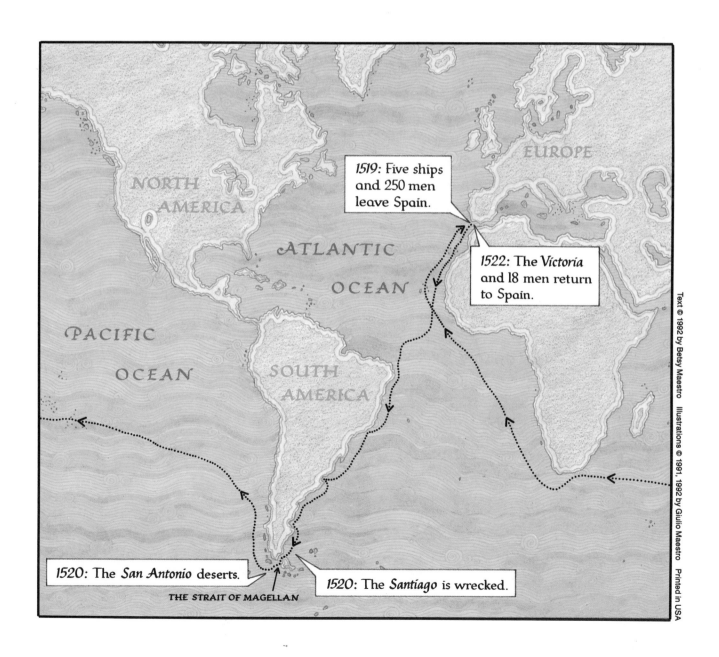

1519: Five ships and 250 men leave Spain.

1522: The *Victoria* and 18 men return to Spain.

1520: The *San Antonio* deserts.

THE STRAIT OF MAGELLAN

1520: The *Santiago* is wrecked.

Text © 1992 by Betsy Maestro   Illustrations © 1991, 1992 by Giulio Maestro   Printed in USA

Focus Activity / Magellan's Voyage

Be a Game Creator

You can do this by yourself or in a small group

Design a board game based on Magellan's voyage. The winner will be the ship that returns to the home port first after circling the globe. Any number of possible pitfalls or problems can delay the ships. Any number of lucky breaks can put a ship ahead. You can just plan your game out on paper, or you can actually construct and play it.

You will need to design a game board showing a map of the voyage. The game also needs playing pieces and sets of "pitfall" and "luck" cards. If you actually do construct the game, you should play it a number of times to iron out the problems before writing the rule book.

This game could also be planned and designed as a video or computer game called "Magellan's Quest." Either way, you need to read a little more about Magellan's journey to give you some starting ideas. Then use your imagination. Not everything in your game needs to be based on facts. Make it exciting—the real journey certainly was! Have fun!

◆ ◆

You're the Captain!

You can do this by yourself

Text © 1992 by Betsy Maestro   Illustrations © 1991, 1992 by Giulio Maestro   Printed in USA

Focus Activity/ Voyages of Columbus

◆ ◆
You're the Captain!

You can do this by yourself

You're the captain on one of Columbus's ships on his first voyage across the Atlantic. Keep a ship's log of the journey. Each day you will record the weather conditions and the speed and position of the ship. You must make note of any unusual happenings on board regarding the condition of the ship, the crew, and the food and water supply. You are in charge and will be held responsible for the outcome of the voyage. This log book will be an important record of your trip.

Your log must begin on the day you leave and end with your arrival in the New World. You will have to pretend that the voyage lasts for only two or three weeks. Since the actual trip took months, it would be difficult to write entries for so many days. Use as much factual information as you can find. Use your imagination to fill in the details.

Remember that the king and queen will read this—so be careful about what you say!

◆ ◆

Hire the Crew

You can do this by yourself or with one or two partners

Text © 1992 by Betsy Maestro   Illustrations © 1991, 1992 by Giulio Maestro   Printed in USA

Focus Activity / Voyages of Discovery

◆ ◆

Hire the Crew

You can do this by yourself or with one or two partners

It is your job to hire a crew for a voyage of discovery in the year 1500. How many men will you need to hire? What positions will you have to fill? You will need to find out about the important jobs of pilot and master. Think of all the other jobs that need to be done aboard ship for the many months that you will be at sea. Food preparation, medical care, and ship repair are only a few of the many necessary tasks.

Try to find the information that you need at the library. Then you can expand on that information by using your imagination. Give the captain a list of your proposed crew members and their duties for his approval.

Remember that a good crew is essential for a successful voyage. Think ahead. Once you are at sea, it will be too late!

◆ ◆ ◆
Present a TV Special

Do this in a small group

Focus Activity / Navigation

Present a TV Special

Do this in a small group

You are making a TV documentary on navigation at the time of Columbus. You will be explaining celestial navigation and showing how Columbus used the stars to guide him. You will be showing the navigational instruments used at that time and explaining how they worked. You can show illustrations of these from books or you can make your own drawings or posters. Perhaps you can make your own compass or astrolabe. Use your visual aids during your talk. Each member of the group should have a part in the program. You can record your presentation using a camcorder, or you can present it "live."

Start by doing some reading about early navigation. Then make your props and plan your show. Write out what everyone will say. Try adding some touches of humor so that your show will be fun to watch. After a few rehearsals, you'll be ready for television!

◆ ◆

Travel Back in Time

You can do this by yourself or with a partner

Focus Activity / European Life in 1492

◆ ◆
Travel Back in Time

You can do this by yourself or with a partner

Pretend that you have invented a time machine. You go back in time and find yourself in a European city in the year 1492. When you return, you are asked to write a magazine article about your adventure. Tell about all the things you saw. Include some description of the buildings, transportation, and the clothing people wore. What kind of food did you eat? Were there schools? Stores? What did people do if they became ill? You will need to do some reading to collect information about life at that time. You will also need to use your imagination to add interesting details.

After you write your article, draw some pictures to go with it. You didn't have your camera along, so you will have to depend on your memory. Share your article with the rest of the class. You can make copies for them or you can read it aloud.

What do you think are the biggest changes in people's way of life between then and now? What has caused these changes? Which time period would you rather live in? Why? These are things to think about and perhaps discuss with your class. Ask them what they think.

◆ ◆ ◆

Explore a Sailing Ship

Do this with a partner or a small group

Focus Activity / Sailing-Ship Design

Explore a Sailing Ship

Do this with a partner or a small group

By about 1500, European sailing vessels were designed to make long voyages across the Atlantic. Although not all these ships were exactly the same, they had many similar features. Do some reading and research to find out about these ships. Find out about their size and shape. Find out about the sails: their number, size, and shape. What were the sails made of? How did they work? How were the ships constructed? Make a large poster showing one of these ships. Label all of its parts. Be able to explain the construction and the working of the sails. If you have enough time and think you are able, you could construct a model of a ship instead.

Try to find out about the inside of your ship. What was below the deck? Where did the men sleep and eat? Where did they store food and other supplies? How did they keep animals on board? Make a second poster showing an interior (inside) view of your ship. Label the different areas to show what they were called and what they were used for. If you have built a model, you can leave one side open to show the interior view.

Share your information with the class. Display your posters or your model.

◆ ◆

Play Discovery Trivia

You can do this with a partner or in a group

Text © 1992 by Betsy Maestro   Illustrations © 1991, 1992 by Giulio Maestro   Printed in USA

Concluding Activity / Trivia Game

◆ ◆

Play Discovery Trivia

You can do this with a partner or in a group

Make a new set of question cards to go with your favorite "trivia" game. Use the material in *The Discovery of The Americas*, including the "Additional Information" section at the back, for your questions. Try to make about fifty cards. Put the questions on the front and the answers on the back. You can use your cards with the board and playing pieces of your trivia game. You can use your cards in place of just one category, such as history, or you can include a number of categories on your cards, such as geography or famous people. If you need more items for a particular category, you can use other books as well. You should try to match the level of difficulty of the trivia game you have and are used to playing. Some questions can be harder or easier than others. You want everyone to be able to answer some questions correctly. Other questions can be real stumpers—maybe only a few kids will know the answer.

Try out your cards. Play a few games. Let other people play. See how your cards work out. You may have to make a few changes if there are problems.

Concluding Activity / Trivia Game

Make a Treasure Map

You can do this by yourself or with a partner

Text © 1992 by Betsy Maestro   Illustrations © 1991, 1992 by Giulio Maestro   Printed in USA

Focus Activity / Natural Resources Mapmaking

31

◆ ◆

Make a Treasure Map

You can do this by yourself or with a partner

Many explorers came to the New World in search of treasure. The treasure was not always what they expected. The New World was rich in natural resources. Some were valuable minerals, such as gold and silver. But some other natural resources, such as timber and fish, turned out to be just as valuable. What other natural resources existed in the New World? Find out what they were and where they were located.

Make a map of the Americas. Show where the natural resources were most plentiful by marking them on your map. Some may be found in a number of different places. Make a key for your map, using a different symbol for each resource. Make your map large and colorful.

Are there some resources that were plentiful in 1500 but are scarce now? Are there some natural resources that were not known in 1500 but are now used? How did the native peoples use the resources of the land? Contrast this with what the Europeans did when they arrived. Be able to discuss your answers when you share your map with the class.

Build a City

Do this in a small group

Text © 1992 by Betsy Maestro   Illustrations © 1991, 1992 by Giulio Maestro   Printed in USA

Focus Activity / Ancient American Cultures

Build a City

Choose one of the ancient cultures mentioned on page 46 of *The Discovery of The Americas*. Do some reading to learn as much as you can about the way these people lived. Find out about their daily existence. What kind of houses did they have? Did they build cities? Smaller settlements? Did they include temples, palaces, or other large buildings? How did they plant their crops? Did they build roads?

Plan and construct a model of a city or settlement. Include a number of buildings and show some of the area around them to indicate the terrain and crops. You may use whatever materials are available. Clay, wood, cardboard, and papier-mâché are a few possibilities. The illustrations in some of the books you use for reference should help give you some ideas about what the cities or settlements may have looked like. The scale or size is up to you. Your city can be as small as a few shoe boxes or as large as a tabletop. But remember—if you are making this at home, you must be able to fit it through a doorway to get it to school!

Share your finished construction with the class. Be able to tell them about the buildings and how they were used. Be able to tell a little about the people who would have lived in your city or settlement.

Focus Activity / Ancient American Cultures

Find Out What Happened

You can do this by yourself or with a partner

Text © 1992 by Betsy Maestro   Illustrations © 1991, 1992 by Giulio Maestro   Printed in USA

Focus Activity / Magellan's Voyage

Find Out What Happened

You can do this by yourself or with a partner

When Magellan sailed, he had a crew of about 250 men on his five ships. When the *Victoria* returned to Spain, only eighteen men were aboard. What happened to the rest of the men? Why did so few survive? Do some research and try to find out what happened to those men who did not return home. It is not possible to account for each one, but it should not be hard to discover many of the perils that befell these men. They did not all perish at the same time or for the same reason.

Write a short report of your findings. Include as many known and possible hazards as you can find or guess at. Try to describe some of the awful experiences these sailors faced. Share your findings with the class.

◆ ◆ ◆

Write a Speech

Do this by yourself

Focus Activity / Leadership Speech

Write a Speech

Do this by yourself

You are the leader of a group of people living in the New World. Europeans have recently arrived on your shores. You know that more will be coming and that their arrival will bring about many changes for your people. What will happen to you and to them? What should you say to your people?

Do some reading so that you will know a little more about what happened to the native peoples when the Europeans came. Then write a speech that you will deliver to your people. Talk about what you think the future holds. Are you positive or negative about what lies ahead? What should your people do? What *can* they do?

Deliver your speech to your class. Ask for their opinions and reactions. Do they agree with what you said?

◆ ◆
Invent Your Own Folktale

You can do this by yourself or with a partner

Focus Activity / Native American Culture

◆ ◆

Invent Your Own Folktale

You can do this by yourself or with a partner

Write an original Native American folktale or legend. Read some of these tales and legends before you try to write your own. Many of them were told to help explain natural events such as the rising and setting of the sun or the changing of the seasons. Many Native American ideas and beliefs were included in these stories. The stories were told again and again and were often acted out in ceremonies and rituals.

Use your own ideas to explain some natural event or mystery. Your explanation should not be based on modern scientific knowledge. Long ago, people did not have that knowledge. So they found simple explanations based on more primitive and magical thinking. Try to do that in your story. Draw a picture for your legend or folktale and share it with the class.

If your class likes to perform plays, you may want to turn your story into a play later. You could even make costumes and scenery for it!

◆ ◆

Solve a Mystery!

You can do this by yourself or with a partner

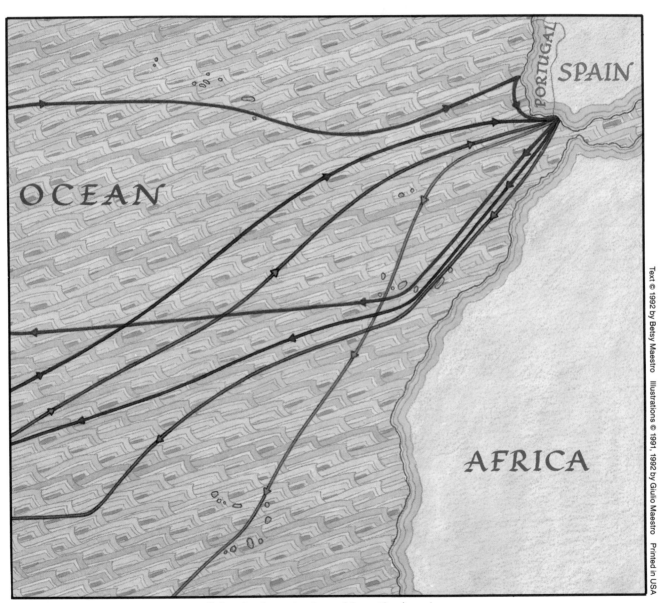

Columbus's routes to and from the Americas

Text © 1992 by Betsy Maestro   Illustrations © 1991, 1992 by Giulio Maestro   Printed in USA

Focus Activity / Christopher Columbus

◆ ◆

Solve a Mystery!

You can do this by yourself or with a partner

If you look at the map showing the routes of the four voyages of Christopher Columbus (pages 28–29 of *The Discovery of The Americas*), you will see that there is no line indicating his return from the third voyage. That is because Columbus did not captain that return trip. Why do you think he didn't? What could have happened to Columbus? Was he ill? Did he choose to be a passenger? Do some research and find out. The answers may surprise you. Write down your findings and report them to the class.

Focus Activity / Christopher Columbus

◆ ◆ ◆

Mutiny at Sea!

Do this in a group of 4 to 8 people

Text © 1992 by Betsy Maestro   Illustrations © 1991, 1992 by Giulio Maestro   Printed in USA

Focus Activity / Mutiny Role Playing

Mutiny at Sea!

Do this in a group of 4 to 8 people

When the going got rough aboard ship and no land was in sight and the journey seemed endless, crews often got angry and restless. Sometimes, if conditions were bad enough, a mutiny or rebellion would erupt. The men wanted to take command of the ship and head for home.

Do some reading about this. Then break up into two equal groups. One group should represent the hired crew, and the other group should represent the leaders on board. Think about what grievances the members of the crew have. Why are they angry? Why do they want to take over the ship? What is their plan? Think about what problems the leaders face. How will they handle the angry crew?

Use your imaginations to plan what your side will say and do when you meet. Then have the two sides confront each other. Let each side have a fair chance to give their views. Experiment a little and see what the outcome of this (nonviolent!) struggle will be. Then perform your confrontation for the class. See how they react. Whose side are they on? Who is right and who is wrong?

◆

Change History

You can do this by yourself or with a partner

Whole-Book Activity / Critical Thinking

Change History

You can do this by yourself or with a partner

The course of history could have been different if just one small event had happened differently or not at all. Suppose the Vikings had stayed in North America. What if Ferdinand and Isabella had said no to Christopher Columbus? What if Magellan had not been killed?

Make a list of at least ten "what ifs." Then, for each one, make up one or two possible other outcomes. How did your small change alter history?

◆ ◆

Visit China

You can do this by yourself or with a partner

Text © 1992 by Betsy Maestro   Illustrations © 1991, 1992 by Giulio Maestro   Printed in USA

Focus Activity / Chinese Inventions

Visit China

You can do this by yourself or with a partner

Pretend that you are Marco Polo and you have arrived in China. The Chinese have invented things that are unknown in Europe. You are amazed by many things you have never seen before. Write a letter home to Italy telling about these new ideas.

Do some reading to find out about the things that were invented in China. Find as many as you can to put in your letter. You will be surprised by many of them. Which ones did Marco Polo take back to Italy with him?

Perhaps you can draw a few pictures to go with your letter. That would help your friends at home to understand how these fascinating inventions actually work.

What if Marco Polo visited our modern world? Which of our inventions would he find most interesting?

◆ ◆ ◆

Make a Mural

You can do this in a small group or with your whole class

Text © 1992 by Betsy Maestro   Illustrations © 1991, 1992 by Giulio Maestro   Printed in USA

◆ ◆ ◆

Make a Mural

You can do this in a small group or with your whole class

A mural is a large picture to be shown on a wall. It is often long and it can show many scenes. Everyone in the class or in your group can work on some part of your classroom mural. If you have a small group, you may not want to make your mural very large. Probably 3 feet high by 5 feet long would be a good size. If the whole class will be working together, your mural could be as long as a whole wall somewhere in your school.

Your mural will show the important events from the book *The Discovery of The Americas*. It will be about the discovery of the Americas. At one end (the left side) show the first people arriving in the New World. Then show the other important events. Make a special picture for each event. At the end of the mural, on the far right side, show the ship *Victoria* coming home after traveling around the world.

Plan the mural in pencil. Figure out how many drawings you will have. Then you can see how much space you have for each one. Draw each picture lightly in pencil first. Then paint each drawing in bright colors.

When your mural is finished, invite the whole school to view your great work of art!

◆ ◆ ◆

Where Were the Women?

You can do this by yourself or in a small group

Focus Activity / Role of Women

Where Were the Women?

You can do this by yourself or in a small group

Everyone will notice that there are practically no women mentioned in *The Discovery of The Americas* or other books about the discovery of the Americas. There were plenty of women around in those days. But where were they? What were they doing? Do some poking around in the library and some thinking of your own about this. See if you can find out more about the role of women during this period in history. Compare some different societies in different places around the world.

See if you can find out or guess why there were no women explorers in those days. What important things were women doing? Find some examples of women who broke tradition and managed to have unusual lives for their times.

Why are the lives of women so different in the modern world? Are there some places where the role of women has not changed? Could a woman have discovered America? What would she have been like? Report your findings to the rest of the class.

Focus Activity / Role of Women

◆ ◆ ◆

Hold a Debate

Do this in a group of 6 to 10 people

Text © 1992 by Betsy Maestro   Illustrations © 1991, 1992 by Giulio Maestro   Printed in USA

Whole-Book Activity / New-World Debate

Hold a Debate

Do this in a group of 6 to 10 people

Was the European discovery and exploration of the New World a good thing or a bad thing? What was good, or positive, about it? What was bad, or negative, about it?

Plan a debate. Make two teams with at least three people on each side. One group should be prepared to argue that the arrival of Europeans was a good thing. Perhaps they will represent the views of the Europeans themselves. The other team should argue that the arrival of the Europeans was a bad thing. This team may want to represent the views and feelings of the native peoples.

Each group should do research and decide what they will say to present and defend their side of the argument. Have discussions as a group to help prepare for the debate. Each person on the team should have something to say.

The actual debate should last about thirty minutes, with each side having fifteen minutes to present its arguments. Your teacher can be the moderator, who will introduce you, announce the order in which you will speak, and tell you when your time is up. The rest of your class will judge the debate. It will be up to them to decide which team was most convincing and why.

◆ ◆

Put On a Play

Do this in a group of 4 to 8 people

Whole-Book Activity / Writing and Performing a Play

Do this in a group of 4 to 8 people

Write a short, one-act play about a real or imagined event suggested by *The Discovery of The Americas*. Some actual events could be the Vikings' landing in Vinland, the arrival of Marco Polo in China, or the death of Magellan. Some imaginary events could show the Mayas building a ship and landing in Europe, Japanese fishermen becoming shipwrecked off the coast of South America, or Saint Brendan landing in the New World. These last two events may really have happened; but since no one knows for sure, you will have to imagine what might have occurred.

Besides using your imagination, you will need to do some reading so that you can make your dramatization seem real. Plan your story line. What will happen in your play? Give each person in your group a role to play and write out what each one will say.

If you're working in a large group, each person should have a job. Probably not everyone can be an actor. But someone has to write out the words, others can make simple scenery, and some might make costumes. Even if there are only a few of you, you can make some scenery or costumes if you wish, but you don't have to. Keep it simple and fun!

Have some rehearsals and try to learn your parts by heart. It will probably help to have one person be the director. When you are ready, perform your play for your class or school.